MY BOOK
WORKBOOK

ENGLISH EXPERIENCES

Janet Gonzalez-Mena

Illustrated by Hari Walner

 NATIONAL TEXTBOOK COMPANY • Lincolnwood, Illinois

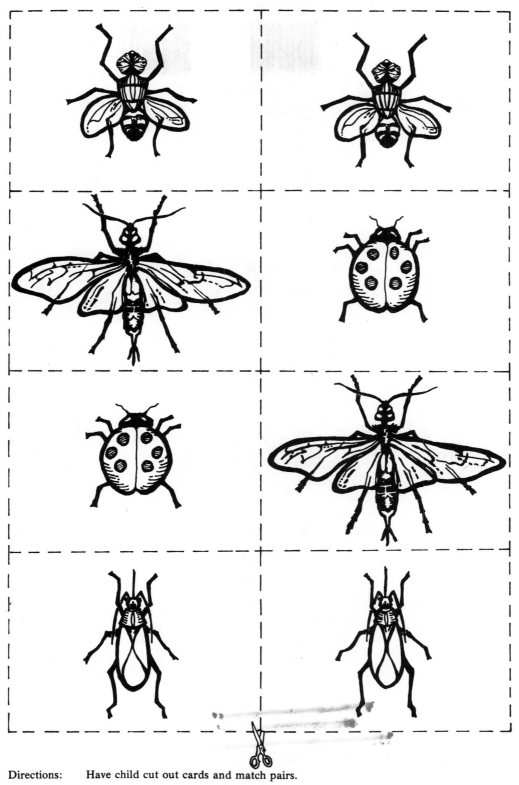

Directions: Have child cut out cards and match pairs.

FLOWER CANDY CANE COFFEE FIRE

ONION PERFUME EGGS FRYING LEMON

SMELLS I LIKE

Directions: Help child circle the smells he likes. Add more smells to the bottom if he can think of any.

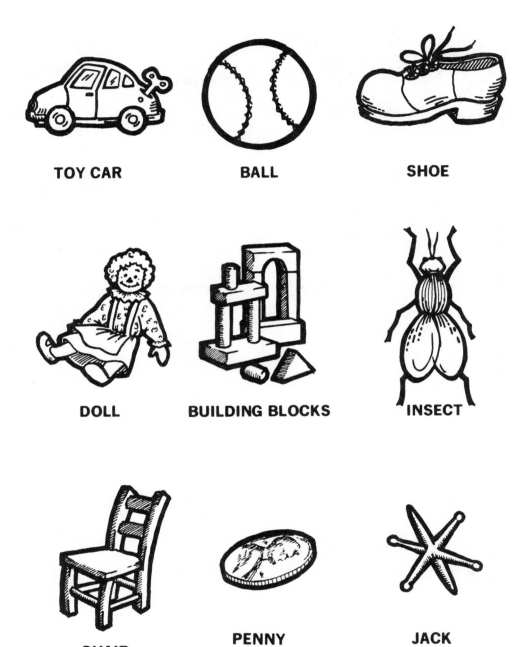

TOY CAR

BALL

SHOE

DOLL

BUILDING BLOCKS

INSECT

CHAIR

PENNY

JACK

TOYS

Directions: Help child circle all items which are toys.

BIG SHOE   **LITTLE SHOE**

BIG FOOT   **LITTLE FOOT**

FEET AND SHOES

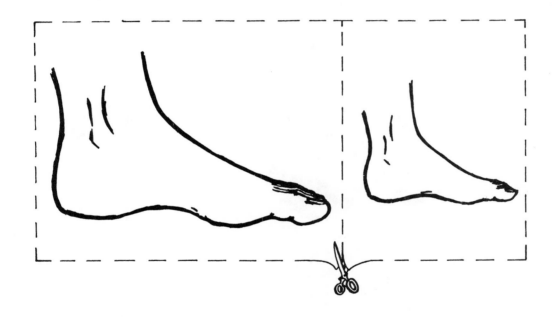

Directions: Help child cut out feet, compare with shoe sizes, match and paste on preceding page.

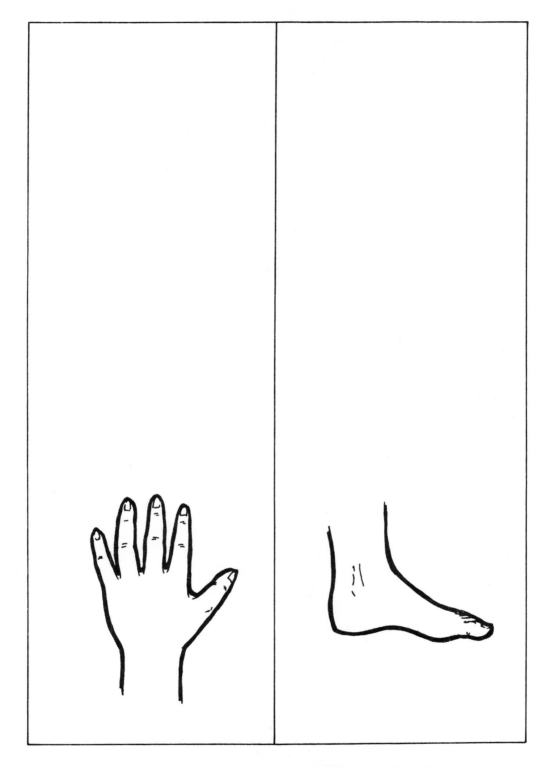

THINGS THAT GO ON HANDS   **THINGS THAT GO ON FEET**

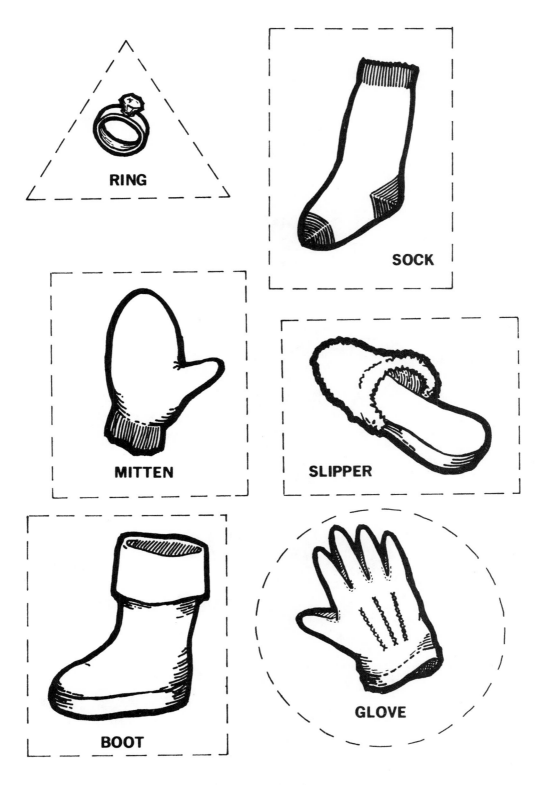

RING

SOCK

MITTEN

SLIPPER

BOOT

GLOVE

Directions: Ask child to cut out all items, sort and paste on preceding page.

A FACE

Directions: Ask child to draw a face.

WHAT'S MISSING?

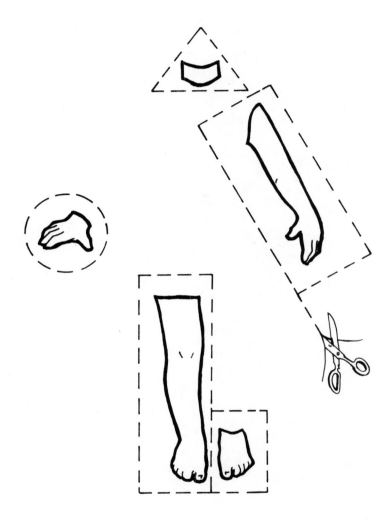

Directions: Ask child to cut out parts of the body. Paste on preceding page.

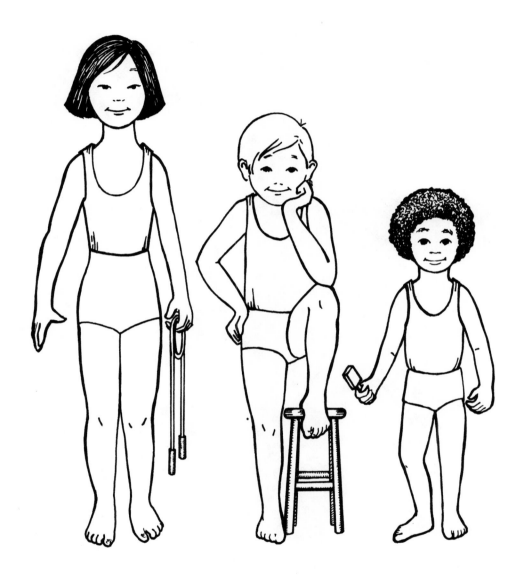

CHILDREN

Directions: Cut out clothes and dress paper dolls on preceding page.

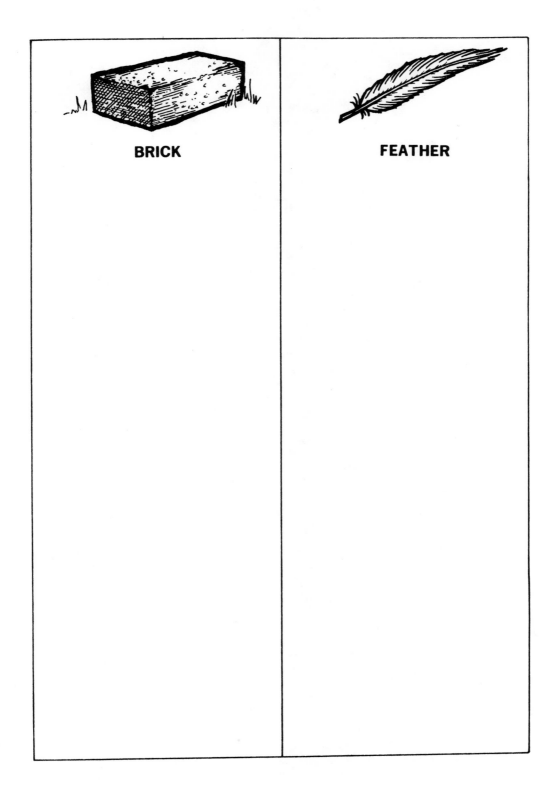

BRICK

FEATHER

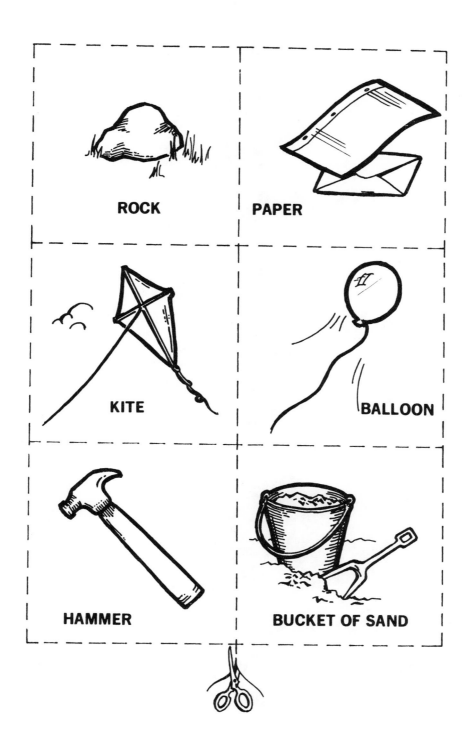

ROCK

PAPER

KITE

BALLOON

HAMMER

BUCKET OF SAND

Directions: Have children cut out pictures. Discuss which things are heavy and which are light.
Have them sort and paste heavy things under the brick and light things under feather
on preceding page.

Directions: Draw a ball going *over* the hill, *on top of* the slide, *under* the bench.

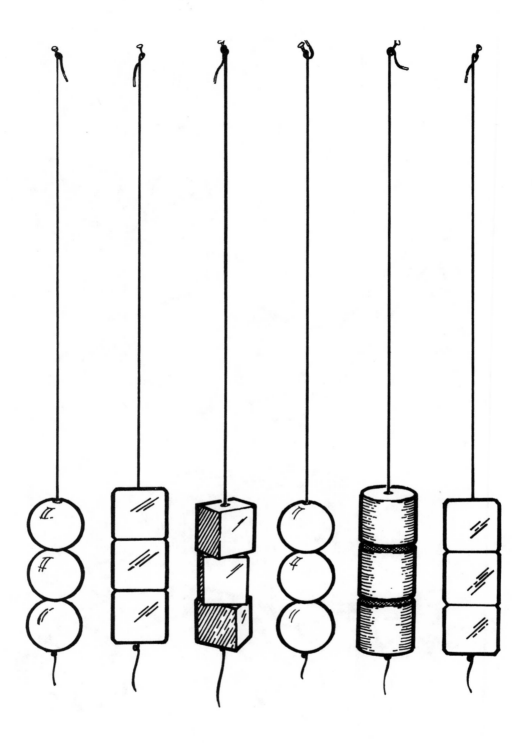

Directions: Ask child to use crayons to add more beads of the same color to each string.

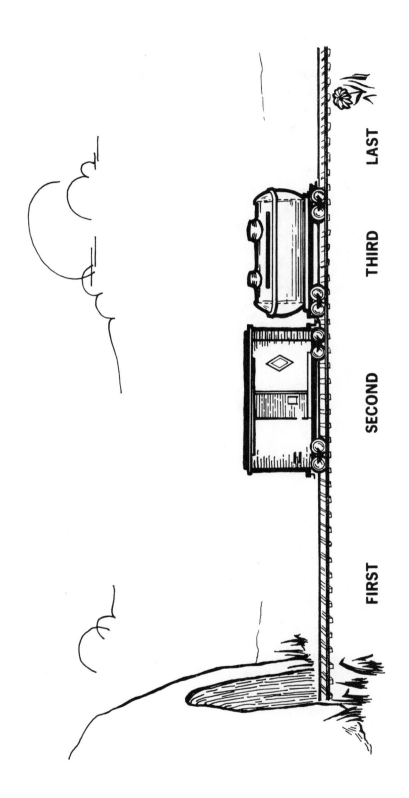

FIRST SECOND THIRD LAST

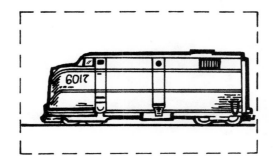

Directions: Tell child train on preceding page is going into the tunnel. He is to paste the engine on the front and the caboose on the end.

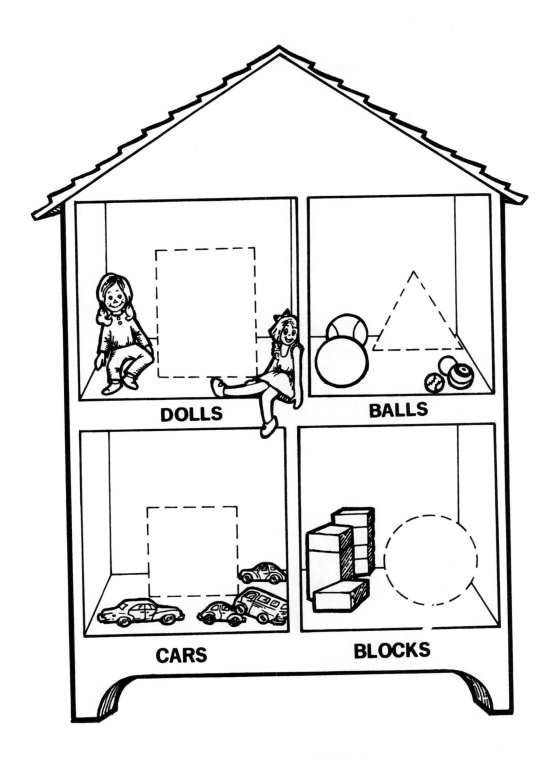

DOLLS

BALLS

CARS

BLOCKS

WHAT'S MISSING?

DOLL

BALL

BLOCK

CAR

Directions: Have child cut toys out and paste on shelves where they belong on preceding page.

ROCK

HARD THINGS

PILLOW

SOFT THINGS

Directions: Give child variety of collage materials representing hard and soft (beans, cotton, felt, gravel, etc.). Ask child to sort and glue.

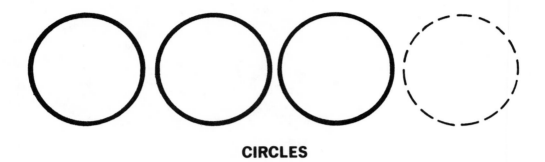

CIRCLES

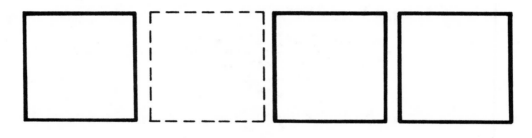

SQUARES

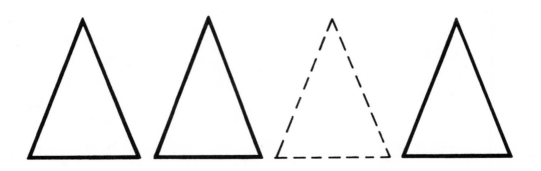

TRIANGLES

CIRCLE

SQUARE

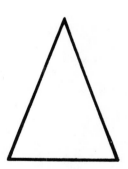

TRIANGLE

Directions: Have child cut shapes out and match them to the shapes on preceding page. Have
him paste them where they belong.

LONG   SHORT

BIG   LITTLE

SQUARE   ROUND

HARD   SOFT

Directions: Ask child to circle the toy he likes best of each pair. Then ask him to say something about that toy.

Directions: Have child cut out baby animals. Have him paste each baby with its own family on the preceding page.

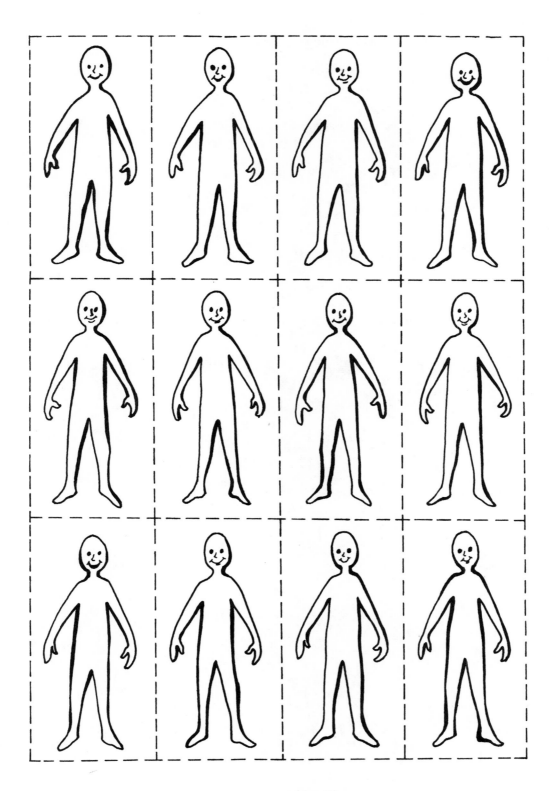

Directions: Have child cut out the same number of figures as he has members in his family. Have him paste them on a blank sheet and say who they are. Label.

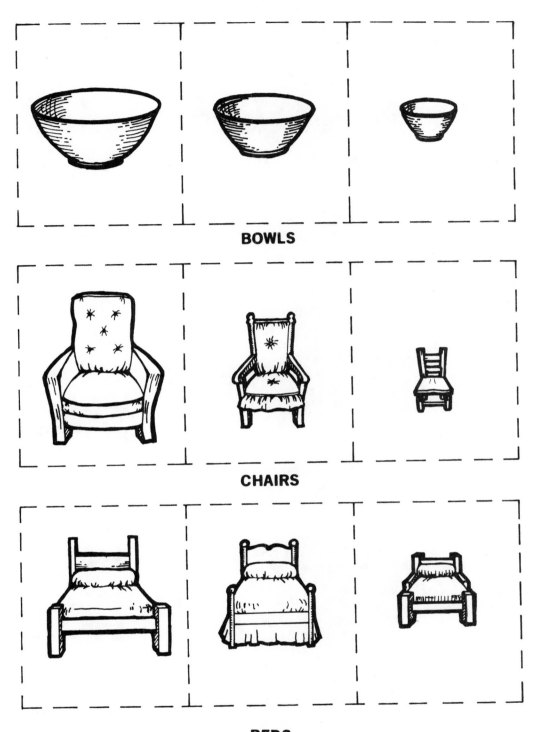

BOWLS

CHAIRS

BEDS

Directions: Have child cut out objects and paste on page, classifying by size.

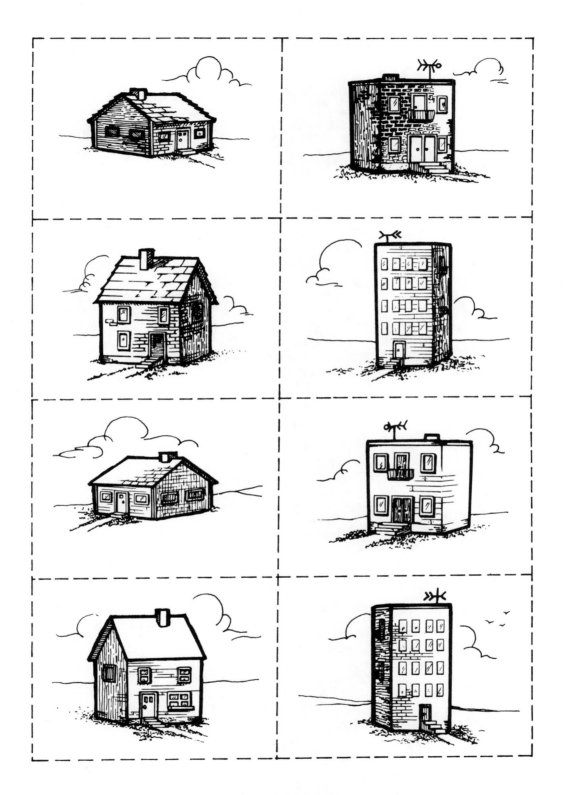

Directions: Have child cut out cards, classify by attributes.

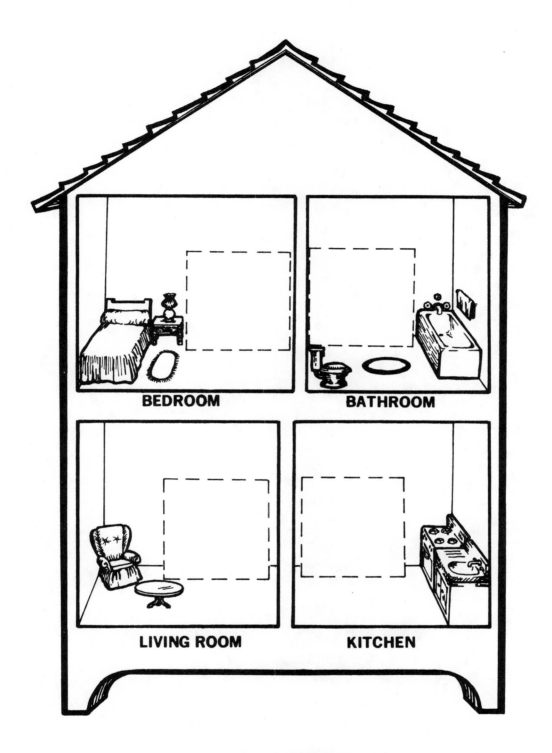

BEDROOM

BATHROOM

LIVING ROOM

KITCHEN

DOLL HOUSE

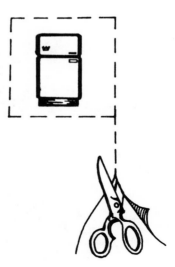

Directions: Have child cut out furniture and paste in proper rooms on preceding page.

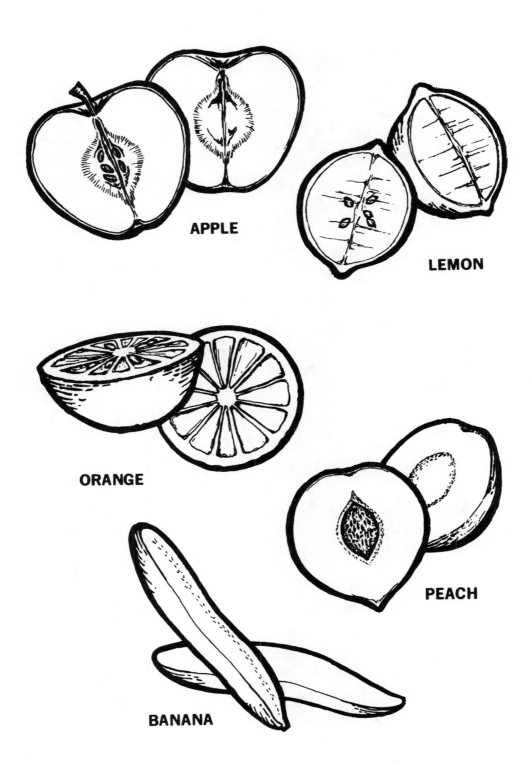

APPLE

LEMON

ORANGE

PEACH

BANANA

Directions: Have child draw seeds in fruit which have no seeds. Point out differences in seeds.

Directions: Tell child to give both children sunflower seeds in their hands. Give one child more
than the other. Let child draw in with crayon, felt pen or pencil.

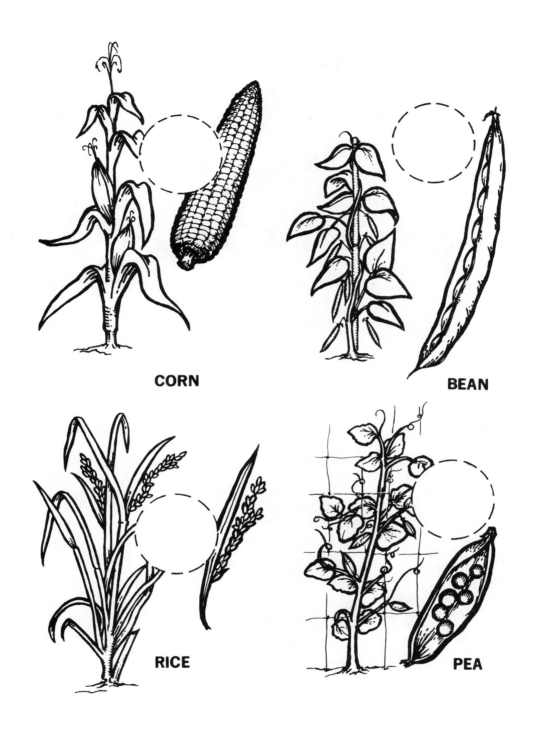

CORN

BEAN

RICE

PEA

SEEDS WE EAT

CORN

BEAN

RICE

PEA

Directions: Tell child to cut seeds out and paste them by the plant they grow on.

POPCORN POPPING

Directions: Ask the child to draw the popcorn popping. Talk with him about the location of the pieces of popcorn in relationship to the pan.

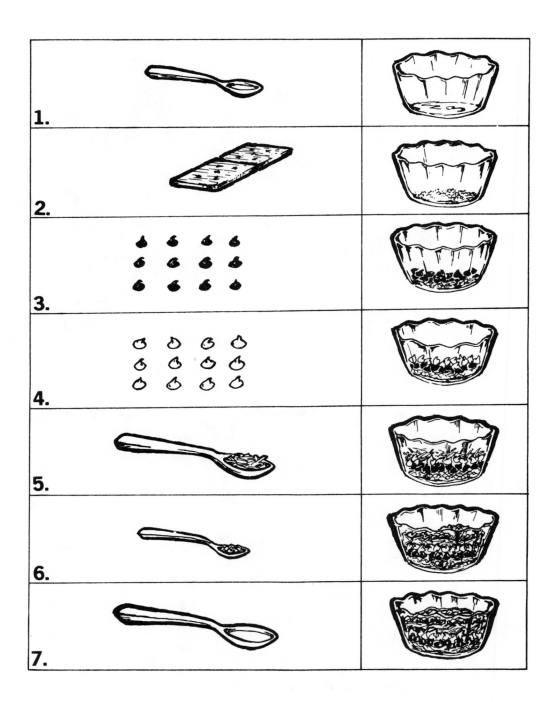

STEPS TO MAKE SEVEN LAYER COOKIE

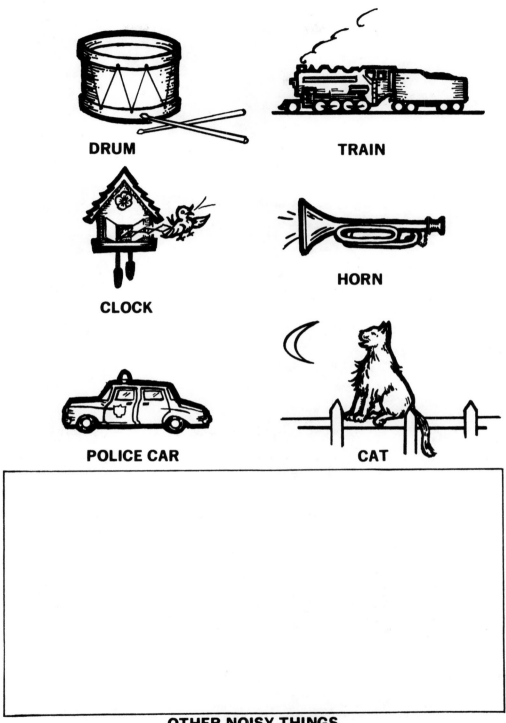

DRUM

TRAIN

CLOCK

HORN

POLICE CAR

CAT

OTHER NOISY THINGS

Directions: Ask child to circle the object that makes the noise that he likes best. Ask him to add his own drawings of things that make noise to the bottom.

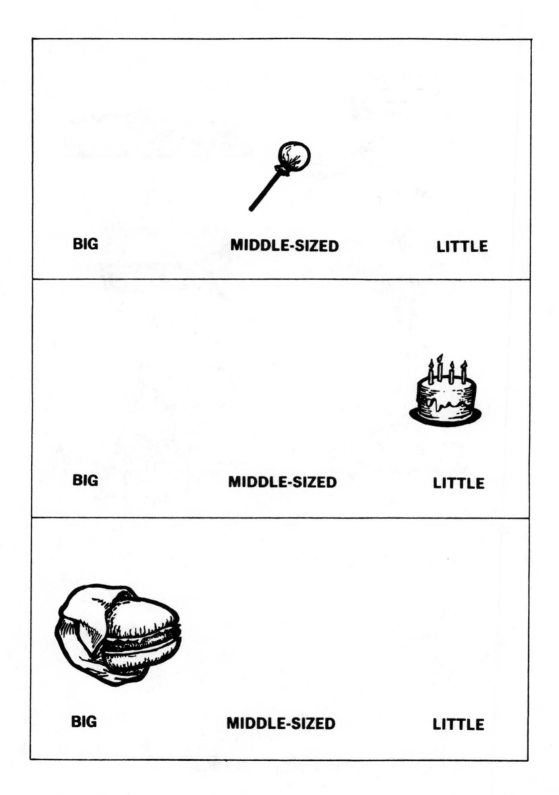

BIG   **MIDDLE-SIZED**   LITTLE

BIG   **MIDDLE-SIZED**   LITTLE

BIG   **MIDDLE-SIZED**   LITTLE

Directions: Child is to cut pictures and paste on preceding page by size.

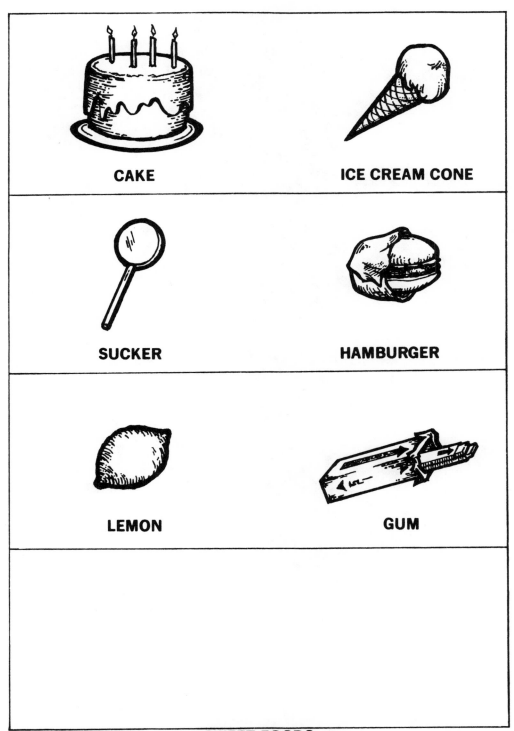

CAKE	**ICE CREAM CONE**
SUCKER	**HAMBURGER**
LEMON	**GUM**

SWEET FOODS

Directions: Ask child to circle foods which taste sweet. Encourage him to draw his own at bottom.

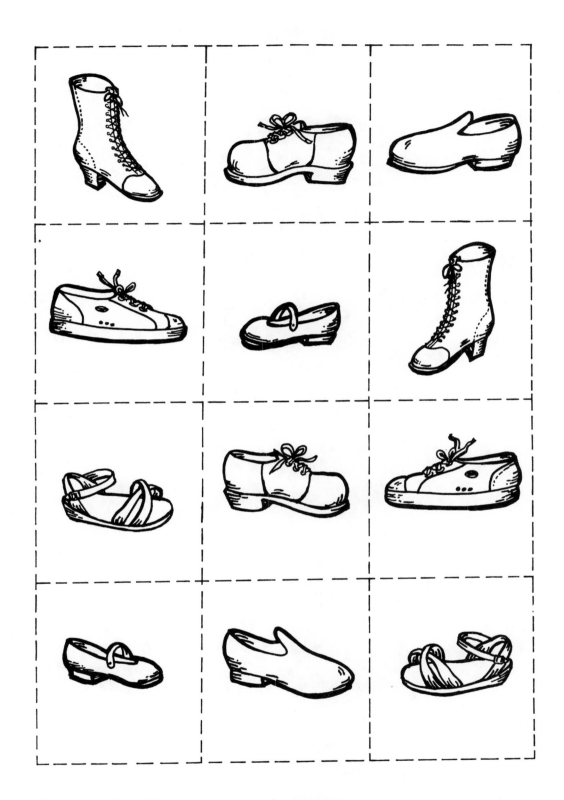

Directions: Have child cut cards, match and paste on page.

MY COMMENTS

_____

_____

Directions: Ask the child to say something about this picture. Write down whatever he says.

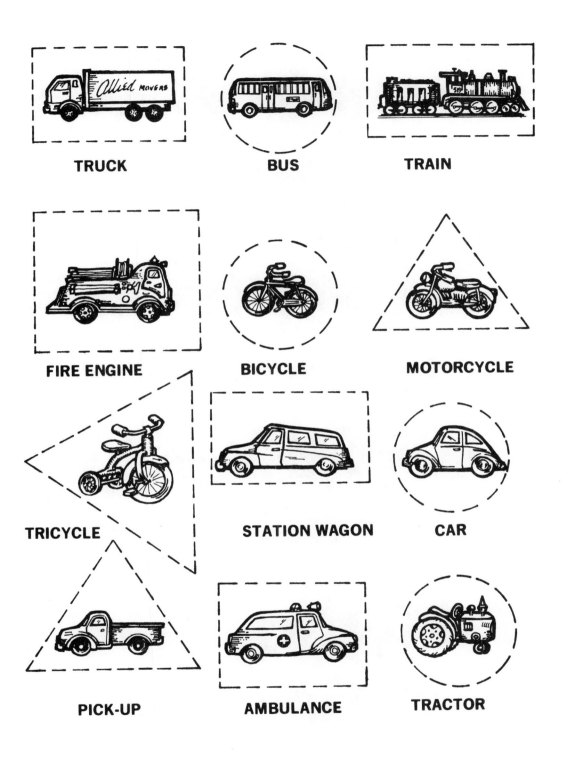

TRUCK

BUS

TRAIN

FIRE ENGINE

BICYCLE

MOTORCYCLE

TRICYCLE

STATION WAGON

CAR

PICK-UP

AMBULANCE

TRACTOR

Directions: Have child cut out pictures of those vehicles the class actually saw on the walk around the neighborhood. Paste on page. Write down any comments he may make.

THINGS FOUND IN A GROCERY STORE	THINGS NOT FOUND IN A GROCERY STORE

APPLE	BOX OF CEREAL	HOT DOGS
BREAD	MILK	DOG
CORN	EGGS	BANANA
GAS PUMP	STREET LIGHT	PUMPKIN
BATHTUB	CANDY	STOP SIGN

Directions: Have the children cut out all the pictures. Paste on page.

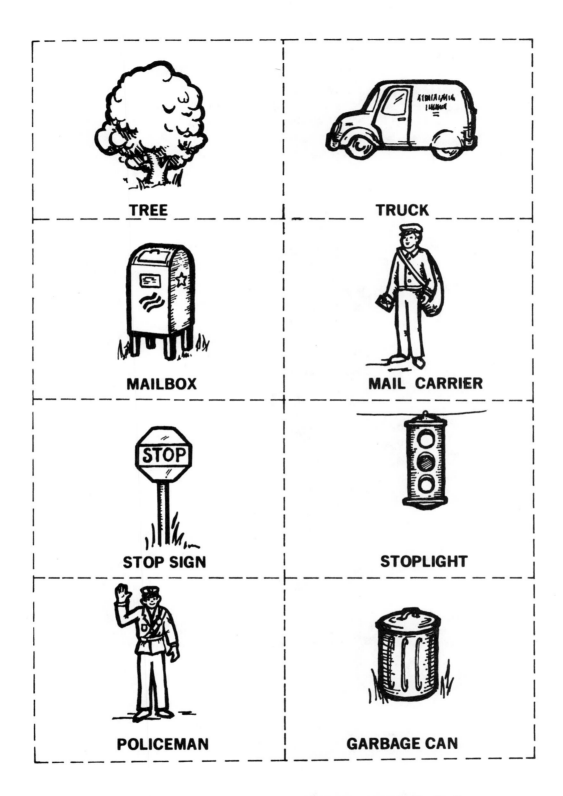

TREE

TRUCK

MAILBOX

MAIL CARRIER

STOP SIGN

STOPLIGHT

POLICEMAN

GARBAGE CAN

Directions: Have child cut out cards to play game described in EXPERIENCE 48.

These blank pages are not included in <u>My Book</u>.
The teacher should supply them in order to complete the child's workbook.